The Breathing Blanket
my signature story

"Greg's signature story demonstrates a powerful struggle throughout his journey in life. He provides living proof of how tremendous will power and listening to your inner self can overcome personal, physical and mental limitations. Greg has become independent, successful and an inspiration to others. His embrace of life and advice in *The Breathing Blanket* is a wonderful example for all to embrace."

Burr J. Smith, retired traffic and safety consultant
– AAA of Michigan, and former educator and police officer

The Breathing Blanket

my signature story

*How
Attitude
and
Listening
Prevail*

Greg Bauer

Grandville, MI

Copyright © 2003 Greg Bauer

Published by
Listen One, a D.B.A. of Greg Bauer and Associates, Inc.
P.O. Box 931
Grandville, MI 49468-0931

Publisher's Cataloging-in-Publication Data
Bauer, Greg.
    The breathing blanket : my signature story : how attitude and listening
    prevail / by Greg Bauer. --Grandville, MI : Listen One, 2003

        p. ; cm.
    ISBN 0-9722353-0-2
        1. Bauer, Greg. 2. Self-realization. 3. Self-actualization (Psychology).
    4. Self-acceptance. I. Title. II. How attitude and listening prevail.

BF637.S4 B38 2003   2002108855
158.1--dc21   0303

Cover design by Kelli Leader
Interior design by Paw Print Media
Book coordination by Jenkins Group, Inc. • www.bookpublishing.com

07 06 05 04 03 • 5 4 3 2 1

Printed in the United States of America

Contents

Acknowledgments

Life is a journey involving many experiences, opportunities, challenges, and accomplishments. I would like to take a moment to thank a few special individuals who have really made a difference in my life and who have had a positive impact on my being able to visualize and experience life's many wonders.

Thank you, Mom and Dad (Gloria and Val), for your countless hours of commitment and belief in my ability to conquer the odds I faced after the crash and also in my ability to grow and mature into adulthood. Also, thank you both for your living commitment to life that served as a positive example for me to follow.

Thank you, brother Ken, for your many years of supportiveness and also for believing that I could overcome the odds of the crash. You've been a true friend and I believe our friendship will endure the test of time.

I want to express a very special thank you to my partner in life, my beautiful, caring, and deeply loving and loved wife, Anna. We've faced life together despite the odds that made themselves known after the crash. Thank you for accepting and loving me in spite of my physical and sometimes painful limitations. Thank you for your love and understanding while we were dating, especially when I told you that doctors had warned me in my later teens and early twenties that the residual bodily effects from the crash would undoubtedly catch up with me by age forty and that I probably would become crippled and die in a wheelchair. I've now exceeded all those specialists' expectations and we've enjoyed a special partnership for over thirty years as a very happily married couple. Thank you my sweetie, my love, for being the quiet inspirational catalyst in my life.

And thank you–the love of my life–for our three great and dynamic children, Matthew, Jennifer, and Angela. They have been and continue to be a very special core of our lives. Not only are we very supportive of their ventures, they are supportive of each other's ventures, and our efforts and accomplishments as well.

Thank you, Matt, my son, for your supportive nature. Also, thank you for your gift of imaginative and intuitive insights and positive outlooks.

Thank you, Jenny, my daughter, for your supportive nature as well. Also, thank you for your gift of sharing and caring for people, including the special way you interact with smaller children.

Thank you, Angela, my daughter, for your supportive nature. I also thank you for your unique gift of caring and understanding with friends and acquaintances.

Thank you, Joel Mayo, my former manager, business colleague, and friend from my former pharmaceutical company days. During these pivotal years of my business mind development, thank you for your guidance and example of what it really takes to be successful in business, from rela tionship building, to persevering, to being accountable, to successfully leading and empowering others.

For the past twelve to fourteen years I've been pursuing a lifetime aspiration that I will work toward for the remainder of my life, and hopefully the legacy will continue far beyond my lifetime. In my efforts as a professional speaker, consultant, and author to help others "utilize the power of effective listening" in their own lives, I continue to be thankful for the assistance, guidance, and support I've received from what I like to call the "University of Professional Speaking." This so-called "university" is a gathering of nationally and internationally represented speakers of the National Speakers Association (NSA) and the Professional Speakers Association of Michigan, now recognized as the National Speakers Association–Michigan Chapter. NSA continues to hold their annual summer conventions with informative and inspiring general sessions and breakout sessions that have helped me tremendously to grow my speaking, consulting, and authorship business. I've learned even more by discussing different aspects of the business with other speaking colleagues out in the hallways between sessions and at meals. This all translates into a "university" hands-on experience, which I'm thankful for being able to receive at NSA's winter workshops on both the east and west coasts.

Thank you, Jerry Conrad, CSP, NSA colleague, and lifetime friend. Thank you for introducing me to the NSA family, both on the Michigan level and at national and international levels. Thank you for your professional, personal, and spiritual support and guidance and sharing of what it takes to be a professional in this industry, which includes forever giving back to and supporting others.

Thank you, Michael Scott Karpovich, CSP, another NSA colleague and dear friend, for so openly sharing the inner components of the wisdom, character, and integrity that it takes to walk one's talk in the business and professional speaking industry.

Thank you, Lee Lebbin, for the longstanding friendship that began with you and your staff as a client, and for the many experiences and accomplishments we have encountered in Toastmasters as a viable and accomplished team for the past six and a half years as officers, with both of us eventually serving as District Governors. Thank you also for the mutual respect we share for each other's goals, accomplishments, and aspirations.

Last, thank you to the countless numbers of volunteers of the Boy Scouts of America for providing me with the fiber it took to build a strong platform for life, a platform that I've been proud to stand and walk on. Thank you for this platform built of strong moral characteristics, accountability, and strength to persevere.

In the Spirit of Sharing with Others

Lord, grant that I may always desire more than I can accomplish.
— MICHELANGELO

*E*ach of us has at least one unique gift. This gift is derived from our ability to share with others our innermost thoughts, emotions, perspectives, creative ideas, and future aspirations. These components collectively express "Who we are" and greatly help to form and reinforce our personal identities. In turn, our identities become our "trademark in life" that helps distinguish us as individuals from everyone else on earth.

When was the last time you took a good hard look at your innermost components, at your unique gift? When was the last time you set aside time to get in touch with who you are as an individual? In other words, when was the last time you *listened to yourself?*

Daily, we each have opportunities that can be turned into accomplishments. It is by listening to ourselves that we recognize these opportunities. Keep in mind that these daily opportunities are probably not gigantic in size, are not readily visible, are not immediately identifiable, and are not easy to categorize. They may well be small in stature, but every day we are confronted by opportunities that can, in time, become major or minor accomplishments.

One way these opportunities may present themselves could include meeting up with an old friend or acquaintance that we haven't seen or heard from in a long time. If this has happened to you, examine how this meeting went. During this reunion, did you take the time and effort to explore how this unique meeting could alter life's possibilities for you or this other individual, or even for both of you? Take a moment to pause and listen to yourself. How could this random meeting enhance the options in your life and/or the many lives you touch daily?

Another way such an opportunity might occur could be concealed among the many daily tasks you perform for others, either at work, at home, or socially. Again, you are encouraged to pause and take the time and effort to listen to your inner thoughts. What are these thoughts trying to convey to you? When are you internally going to schedule taking action on these new dynamic inner thoughts?

Now, let's envision that one day your time on this earth suddenly comes to a catastrophic conclusion. You aren't given any time to get your thoughts, your innermost components, or your affairs in order. Suddenly, your dreams end. Your innermost components cease to exist, and your opportunities for accomplishment are over.

Too many of us live day by day, taking life's opportunities much too lightly, forever thinking these moments will keep flowing like water from a faucet. We almost never consider that the source of the water may just dry up and no longer exist, or that the water line to the faucet may break, either from deterioration or from being bumped in an accident.

If and when this time arrives, how prepared will our minds be to meet the challenges that will confront us? How able will we be to meet these obstacles and overcome the challenges imposed? Will we possess the fortitude to come out of such confrontations even stronger than before they appeared? We surely don't want to become less as individuals after each challenge we encounter.

Our ultimate goal should always be building inner strength, character, and self-esteem. After all, life is a series of events and situations that help make up our everyday personal identity. Unfortunately, as human beings we frequently find ourselves merely existing, with no momentum, floating in a catatonic state.

If this isn't where you want to be, when are you going to start listening to yourself and identifying your innermost components? When are you going to start envisioning those opportunities that will become accomplishments? When are you going to set those opportunities into motion to perpetuate the evolution of further accomplishments?

The sooner we take into our souls and innermost components the realization that life does not last forever, the sooner we will be able to identify our opportunities and transform them into accomplishments.

Ponder the following questions as they pertain to your life:

1. Are you embracing those opportunities that may help improve your life?
2. Are you making choices that are going to inevitably determine your path of life, or are you allowing others or circumstances to determine your path of life and its consequences and outcomes?

What follows in this book is a real-life story–my own real-life story. As a survivor of a drunk-driving crash at the age of two that nearly took my life, that required extensive physical therapy for me to learn to walk and talk again, and that has left me with life-long physical challenges, I truly believe that such opportunities appear on a daily basis. I believe that each of us has the potential to generate and develop opportunities and turn them into real-life accomplishments. This book will help you better understand this concept through the eyes of my real-life experience.

The moment of my own personal confrontation with death occurred suddenly, unexpectedly, and at one of the healthiest times of my life. By all means of common sense, medical knowledge, and emergency response team reactions, I was considered to be dead. It was sudden, unexpected, and apparently final.

This was not a dream or a nightmare–it was all very real. The terror involved in this event was unbelievable. The physical pain was intolerable. The finality of never being able to utilize my innermost components to help express opportunities that would become accomplishments appeared evident.

Focusing on the options, I chose to pursue my dreams, hopes, and aspirations. An overabundant positive attitude emerged to help me overcome what appeared to be monumental challenges and roadblocks that many thought I would never be able to manage.

As I share my personal story with you, feel free to take notes in the margins. Should you observe moments of encouragement that may be of assistance in your own life, I again encourage you to take notes.

My goal is to help you realize your own real-life potentials through utilizing the power of effective listening . . . to *yourself.* To that end, each chapter concludes with a brief section called "Greg's Thoughts for Future Reflecting" that repeats a sentence or phrase used in the chapter that you can reflect on. Each chapter reveals a different phase in my life and how the breathing blanket played an integral role in determining my inner thought processes. The inner ability to listen to myself and actively turn my thought processes into day-by-day self-improvements and self-fulfilling actions became a key element in my evolving into a successful, creative, and contributing individual.

Welcome to my world: "In the spirit of sharing with others, opportunities become accomplishments!"

Chapter One

The Beginning and the End, of Sorts

*Do not let what you cannot do
interfere with what you can do.*
– JOHN WOODEN

My life began as the first son of a struggling, hard-working, proud family. My father was the son of plow farmers in the thumb area of Michigan. In his late teens he entered the conflict of World War II and fought for the freedoms and standards of our nation on the battlefields of Italy. In town after town, he survived the many battles that his unit engaged in and ultimately received the Purple Heart on the field of battle.

My mother's father worked on the assembly line at the Ford factory in Dearborn, Michigan. In her late teens, she went to work for the military's war department in offices in Detroit.

My mother and father were joined together in courtship and, eventually, marriage. They began living the American dream in the post-World War II era. Shortly after their wedding they purchased a house in Detroit. My father became a firefighter with the Detroit Fire Department and my mother became a full-time homemaker.

Opportunities began to become more apparent. It seemed like the harder my parents worked, the more opportunities appeared. My father, established in a career he really liked, was part of a team of firefighters who shared a certain character. As veterans of World War II, they were uniformly tough and rugged individuals. Early on, my father also acquired part-time jobs as a painter and local truck driver during his off-hours as a firefighter.

This was the formation of a generation we today label the "Baby Boomers." In the United States, the land of opportunity and prosperity, the idea of working hard, as well as the need to persevere, was instilled into those who wanted to succeed. After all, these people grew up during the difficult times of a nationwide depression and survived the perils of World War II. Through everyone's dedication to being productive and working long hours, individuals felt a special sense of accomplishment.

My day-to-day exposure to these ideals may help to explain my attitude and stance on succeeding, persevering, and the need to live beyond just surviving in the emerging story.

Born a healthy baby boy, I suffered no complications at birth and no serious diseases in my first two years. At age two, I was a bouncing boy with attentive parents. My birth and early childhood were a highlight of my parents' lives. Producing a healthy child was a real accomplishment. In addition, my parents by then had purchased a new house and piece by piece they were very nicely furnishing it. Life was now full and rewarding, though hard work would always be inevitable.

This was an evolutionary time in my life, as it is for all toddlers. According to the recollections of my parents, relatives, and friends who knew me, I would playfully romp around the house and even venture out into the backyard, agile, playful, and adventurous. My life so far was typical, barrier-free from any roadblocks that might prevent me from continuing to grow in the normal sequence of events. In short, I was practicing and performing successfully on my path of life.

The day of the crash was like any other for me and began on an upbeat note for our family. The sun was shining, the birds were chirping, and the quiet of the morning opened to the hustle and bustle of living in the big city of Detroit. My activities that day were quite normal, from eating breakfast and lunch, to playing with my toys, to behaving in a typical two-year-old manner to get my mother's attention, according to the accounts of the day expressed by my parents.

Not only was it fun being two, I was going to be a big brother! My mother was seven months pregnant and soon I was going to have a new companion. The family's expectations were high and this cherished pregnancy was viewed as another accomplishment; another reward for all their hard work and struggles was about to appear.

At two years of age, I understood that my father was coming home for dinner and that after dinner we were going to get in the car and travel somewhere in the city. So, once the dinner table was cleared and the dishes were washed, we ventured out to the car sitting in the garage.

It was now evening. The sun was setting and intermittent light rain was beginning to fall. It was a bit damp out, not as warm as it had been in the afternoon sunshine. I was sitting in the back seat and occasionally shifting from one side of the car to the other to take advantage of seeing the city. In that day and age, the early 1950s, no seat belts, child restraints, or car seats existed to prevent me from moving around or boosting me up to obtain a better view. My pregnant mother sitting in the front passenger seat of the car, likewise, wore no seatbelt or restraint.

On our way home after our evening adventure, we came to a stoplight that had just turned red. There we sat, positioned in the left lane prepared to make a left-hand turn when the light turned green. It was dark now and all the cars had their headlights on, including ours.

Suddenly, out of the corner of his eye in the rear-view mirror, my father noticed a vehicle rapidly approaching in the distance. He noticed that it wasn't slowing down. In fact, it almost seemed to be speeding up. It wasn't veering to the left or right to avoid us, but seemed to be coming head on, like an approaching single-engine freight train.

The reflexes in my father's mind took hold and he immediately grasped the steering wheel with his strong firefighter hands. He yelled, "Hang on," as the approaching car came closer. My mother attempted to support herself.

The approaching vehicle proceeded to ram into the rear bumper of our car at an impact speed of around fifty miles per hour. No visible brakes were applied and no skid marks showed on the pavement to demonstrate that the approaching vehicle had made any effort to slow down.

The thrust, the momentum generated from this impact, was unbelievable. It seemed as though our lives were now in a state of suspended animation. They were racing, yet in slow motion, all at the same time.

The horrific impact ejected my mother from the passengers' door onto the damp cold pavement, flinging her pregnant body several feet from the car. She was badly bruised and lay there unable to move with fractured bones.

The momentum of this chain reaction of events caused my father's hands to become one with the steering wheel. They so tightly clenched the wheel that they acted like a vice embracing a piece of wood. His hands were bleeding, and his face and body endured numerous cuts and bruises.

Amongst the momentum of the situation and the crashing of the metal and the shattering glass emerged my two-year-old body. I was immediately ejected and lifted from the back seat, my little body now in flight with no navigator or pilot to guide it to its final destination. I flew over the front seat and the dashboard and smashed through the thousands of intact glass particles of the windshield. The excruciating and nerve-wrenching pain that my small body endured upon impact during this crash became an intolerable life-altering moment, indeed a definite "landmark" in my life. My mangled body flopped over the front hood of the car several times and landed on the cold, wet, gaseous-smelling pavement. I could not move, for my entire body was completely paralyzed. But fortunately, according to attending medical experts and my parents, I was no longer able to feel any pain. When the firemen and policemen came and assessed the tragic state of circumstances, they placed a large, reddish-brown blanket over my entire body, from head to toe. They considered me to be dead.

The scene smelled of leaking gas from both cars and puddles of water formed from the fire hoses as the firefighters extinguished the flames that had resulted from the tremendous impact. The pedestrians standing around were in a state of shock, and the faces of the policemen investigating the situation and controlling the crowd conveyed sorrow and mournfulness.

From this point forward, neither my life nor that of my parents would ever be the same again. This encounter took on its own identity and was, of course, totally unplanned, unrehearsed, and undesired. It completely altered my path of life.

***

Greg's Thoughts for Future Reflecting

1. *The excruciating and nerve-wrenching pain that my small body endured upon impact during this crash became an intolerable life-altering moment, indeed a definite "landmark" in my life.*
2. *They placed a large, reddish-brown blanket over my entire body, from head to toe.*
3. *From this point forward, neither my life nor that of my parents would ever be the same again.*

Chapter Two

The Breathing
Blanket

*I will say about an optimist—
even when things don't turn out well,
you are certain they will get better.*
— FRANK HUGHES

s this disastrous evening continued to unfold, some truths began to reveal themselves.

My mother, attended to by firefighters and ambulance personnel, was immediately rushed to the hospital where she gave birth to my stillborn baby brother, David, who never survived the impact of the crash. My mother was hospitalized for cuts, bruises, fractures, and shock.

My father's hands, clenching the steering wheel, were unlocked one finger at a time. When he was no longer one with the steering wheel, the firemen helped his bruised, cut, and tormented body from the car. He then proceeded to walk around the car and the crash scene, stumbling aimlessly in total disbelief as to what had occurred.

The driver of the car that crashed into us walked away from the crash pain-free from the high alcohol content in his body. He had been stone cold drunk. Fortunately, he had no passengers in his vehicle.

As my mangled, bruised, motionless, and assumed dead body laid on the wet pavement with the reddish-brown blanket covering me from head to toe, the firemen, policemen, and my now petrified father waited for the coroner to come.

Though I was unconscious, I was apparently literally at the point so many of us think we are at from time to time–the point when we think to ourselves or express to others, "It's over. I give up. I can't go any further."

At this point, each of the following twelve dimensions of total despair that I've personally experienced, observed, and identified over the past five decades would have applied to me at this moment and at many other moments in the years to come.

TWELVE DIMENSIONS OF TOTAL DESPAIR

1. This is it!
2. I can't take it anymore!
3. Life is not worth living anymore!
4. Why try?
5. It's not worth it!
6. I can't do that!
7. I give up!
8. Who cares?
9. I can't go on!
10. Please put me out of my misery!
11. It's impossible!
12. I've totally run out of options!

Thus, the following moments that occurred at the crash scene were shocking to everyone. One of the firefighters who was standing in the proximity of my blanketed body thought he saw the blanket making slight movements. Upon approaching it and examining the motions he thought he saw, he exclaimed in a shocked voice, "The breathing blanket . . . The blanket is *breathing!*" This mysterious breathing blanket was immediately pulled off my face and an ambulance was called, which rushed my limp body to the hospital.

I remained unconscious as tests determined that I was paralyzed from head to toe. As hopeless as this might have appeared, there were numerous positives to this set of circumstances. For starters, I was breathing. My lungs were working. I was in a clean, dry hospital, where my cuts and bruises were being tended to by caring people. The very fact that I was alive was a glimmer of hope. Let's face it, this sure beat the alternative I had been facing back at the crash scene.

However, throughout the next three to four weeks, I lay lifeless, unconscious, and completely paralyzed. The prognosis from the doctors and specialists was that my body and head had endured multiple life-threatening impacts, so many that they determined I would never recover.

In those days, modern science didn't fully understand paralysis and its effects on the human body; the doctors believed my body would eventually give out and I really would die this time.

My father's scars and my mother's bumps, bruises, and broken bones slowly healed, as my parents waited to hear something, anything about my progress. Meanwhile my parents and relatives buried the body of my stillborn brother, David, at a cemetery in Detroit.

The individual least affected by the crash was the drunk driver who caused it. He served no time in jail and merely paid a fine for a traffic violation.

At the end of the fourth week after the crash, a miraculous moment occurred and the left side of my body began to show movement and reflexes. It's as though the Lord came down and said, "Hey kid, snap out of it!" It didn't happen instantaneously, but as the weeks progressed, movement in my left side became more pronounced and I regained consciousness. Eventually, I began uttering sounds and words. With ongoing therapy and rehabilitation over the next several weeks, my left side began to move even more.

My right side was still in a state of paralysis, but it too began to show some movement as the weeks progressed. Throughout the next three years this paralysis dissipated day by day, though my right side never recovered completely and permanent signs lingered that would last forever.

In retrospect, I came to see that reddish-brown breathing blanket as a symbol of hope in my life. It took hold of my very heart and soul and became a glimmer of perpetual light that continues to shine to this day. That dynamic symbol became a living catalyst, not only at this time in my life, but at every other time of my life as well. Because that blanket breathed, life continued to offer choices and possibilities to be discovered, explored, and developed.

I can't say that my recovery or what I've since accomplished in my life came without hard work or sacrifice, but the very thought of the breathing blanket has consistently provided a spark, a ray of sunshine to reach for in challenging days.

That breathing blanket has been a symbol of hope for the past fifty-plus years. I am so grateful for all the opportunities it has offered me in meeting the challenges in my life that I want to offer it as a symbol of hope for you.

The realities of my life and the opportunities that lay ahead slowly began to be formulated in my mind, at first through factual recollections that my parents shared with me between the ages of nine and twelve. Then, when I was thirteen and fourteen, my parents communicated to me their strong emotional recollections to the factual recollections. I now had a pretty clear picture of the crash, how it had affected all of our lives spiritually, emotionally, and physically, and the challenges and limitations both my parents and I would have to meet in the future.

Try to put yourself in the position I was in. Now try to imagine what it would be like to be under that blanket, presumed dead. Lord willing, short of actually dying, don't you find yourself under that blanket every day, figuratively speaking? In our everyday pursuit to overcome and succeed, far beyond the limitations the twelve dimensions of total despair try to put upon us, we each try to evolve from our own blanket, of sorts. This blanket helps to guide us and offers ongoing hope for the future. When we evolve from this blanket of hope, we will succeed at anything we pursue. We can overcome the trap doors and land mines that the twelve dimensions of despair constantly place in our path of life. I encourage you to try to take advantage of the moments you spend under the blanket. Try to listen to the signals permeating from your heart, emotions, and feelings, and listen for the signals derived from others as they share their own life experiences with you.

Like me, you have the opportunity to confront the challenges and roadblocks in your life as you face the daily hurdles that life has to offer. Listen, don't speak, to the direction your own breathing blanket is attempting to guide you toward. Look for the many signs of hope, human prosperity, human generosity, and gifts of God that life has to offer that surround you daily. After all, the many opportunities your path of life has to offer are ultimately determined by your ability to recognize them.

Greg's Thoughts for Future Reflecting

1. *I've totally run out of options.*

2. *It's as though the Lord came down and said, "Hey kid, snap out of it!"*

3. *Listen, don't speak, to the direction your own breathing blanket is attempting to guide you toward.*

Chapter Three

Listen to Yourself

It sometimes seems that intense
desire creates not only its own
opportunities, but its own talents.
— ERIC HOFFER

As I lay limp and unconscious in the hospital after the crash, my mind and body were confronted with taking one of two options. They could both either call it quits or they could move forward with a fervent determination to pursue life. Both my mind and body opted to take the latter path by internally communicating with and listening to each other. Even at age two, one's mind and body are capable of this powerful internal reasoning.

But everyone else was saying this battered, paralyzed, and tormented body of mine was never going to make it. Even the medical specialists looking after my case were saying the odds for my long-term survival were hopeless, let alone my chances for recovery in a halfway decent form.

This would have been a good time for me to just give up, to throw in the towel. First, my body couldn't move, for it was completely paralyzed. Second, my mind was so severely impacted that my memory of how to form words had evaporated. Even after I had regained consciousness, four weeks after the crash, I remained mute. Third, my mind and thought patterns as to how to connect messages from my mind to my bodily functions and movements were at a standstill. Think about it. How much more hopeless could this situation have been? All sources of medical intervention were calling it quits. Also, all of the medical sources had my parents prepared for my inevitable demise. According to my parents' accounts of the aftermath of the crash, it seemed like the entire world around them was prepared for my death to occur suddenly and soon.

Medical experts in today's world say that a mind in the state mine was in is still able to hear verbal communications both unconsciously and consciously. Again, based on my parents' recollection, I was receiving only messages of despair and abandonment. Furthermore, the state of the medical art of dealing with paralysis and brain damage was nowhere near the level of sophistication that exists today. These seemed to be the odds that were stacked against my two-year-old defenseless mind and body that had been attacked by a mindless drunk driver.

As I grew, my parents, Val and Gloria, remained very protective and supportive of my survival and successes in life. However, they frequently reminded me both directly and indirectly of the desperate situation I had experienced at age two. They thought I should live within my physical and mental limitations and be content with experiencing a limited life. They never seemed to let go of my almost demise at age two, and never did totally adjust to my desiring and accomplishing my own goals in life. Both my mom, who remained a loyal homemaker and dedicated wife for over forty-five years of marriage until her death from inoperable brain cancer at age seventy-three, and my dad, who retired from the Detroit Fire Department as a lieutenant and pursued a career as a financial consultant until his death from eventual heart failure at age seventy-eight, were too frequently prepared to remind me of my near-death experience.

This reminds me of other close friends and acquaintances of mine who were seemingly unable to accept the next step in their lives. They became immobile and devasted by receiving the raw end of a divorce or the abrupt loss of a job to which they committed their hearts and souls. I, instead, made the choice to respond differently and not put a closure to all my options. Some of my friends have had their minds thrown into neutral by a dramatic event that affected them in high school or college that they couldn't shake off even years later. They quit believing in themselves and even believing in others. The worst is when they isolated themselves from any involvement in the world. I find that to truly be a travesty, not only for these individuals, but also for all of mankind who will miss out on being exposed to their contributions.

I was at this dramatic and climactic point in my own life now, even at age two. How could I ever forget what my parents repeatedly told me? But as the days passed, I found myself drawing from my inner strengths and abilities the desire not only to survive, but an inner determination to succeed.

After my left side began to show movement, the daily exercise and physical therapy programs helped me to become stronger and more coordinated. Eventually a certain amount of strength appeared in my right side as well. Some five or six months after the crash, walking braces were attached to my legs and I wore these twenty-four hours a day for the next three years. These braces, attached to high-rise walking shoes, became part of my daily life. In the beginning I would drag my right foot more than walk on it, but progressively I was able to walk with a limp.

The determination and strength life had to offer me were being soaked up and turned into energy by my tormented body. The doctors, who couldn't believe I had survived the crash, were very supportive of the outcome they were now visualizing. My parents were also very supportive, applauding my each and every small success as they lived with me through each day both in and out of the hospital.

During this period from age two to age five, I also relearned how to verbalize words and sentences in a conversational way. I often stuttered while trying to express those sentences, but the stuttering eventually dissipated as time progressed.

I was not leading a carefree life in these developmentally critical years. Initially, most of my time was spent just trying to survive the crushing physical and mental torment of the crash. Then, the majority of my time was spent trying to see just how far my body and mind could improve with therapy. Last, I began trying to figure out how I was going to ever be able to play and interact effortlessly like "normal" kids seemed to do.

During this period from age two to five, I was under constant rehabilitation. For the first three months after the crash, I found myself in the hospital as a permanent resident with my parents constantly at my side. For the next three years I was periodically in and out of the hospital and doctors' offices receiving rehabilitation. My parents had moments of utter frustration along with moments of day-by-day patience. Sometimes weeks or even months went by without any visible signs of improvement. For my parents, the events of these days became a dominant part of their lifestyle. At times, they became more emotionally involved in this real-life drama than I did, because they were visualizing these events from an adult perspective.

As I mentioned before, I believe that my ability to listen to myself, which gave me the inner strength to not only survive but to succeed, was derived in large part from the atmosphere I was brought up in. From the very day I was born, I believe my parents' way of life and emphasis on determination and perseverance became instilled in me.

A very strong and determined voice inside of me, sometimes whispering and sometimes very effectively shouting, caused me to listen. This process of listening to myself began to be quite evident when I became focused on:

- *Making the most of each day, no matter what negatives or barriers would get in my way.* For instance, after a visit to the doctor's office, my parents were told there was no way they could lengthen my right leg any further and that I would walk with a pronounced limp. That strong and determined inner voice very firmly reminded me that I *could* walk, I *could* move, and my body was still very mobile. The limp? That was merely an inconvenience and a far, far cry from being paralyzed.

- *The great aspects in life that the future had to offer in so many imaginative ways.* For instance, when my parents would start in on yet another conversation with a relative or friend about the crash and its devastating aftermath, my strong and determined inner voice would grab my listening attention and remind me not to linger or cling to the past. The past was done and over, and its events could not be rearranged or redone.

Usually these discussions would take place in the same vicinity or room I was sitting or playing in. I remember that when I took what I was hearing too seriously, I would begin to feel inept and helpless. My inner voice would remind me to focus on the future and how I was going to structure the many possibilities for the many tomorrows ahead.

■ *The very fact that nothing comes easily or automatically just because we wish it to be true.* To get ahead, I found that I had to struggle, persevere, and be more competitive than the rest of the kids I played with. For instance, from the ages of seven to eleven when my friends and I would show up at the school ball field to pick up teams for playing sandlot baseball, I knew that I was not as athletically inclined, as fast, or as coordinated as most of them. I learned to accept that status, but I continued coming back to play. I was always picked to play some position (most of the time right field or pitcher, as those positions did not require a lot of fast movement), and I enjoyed being active. Furthermore, I was always picked last, but my inner voice kept telling me not to focus on that, but instead to focus on the fact that I always *was* picked to play.

Each of us possesses the inner power to slow down and listen to ourselves. When we do this, we give ourselves the ability to grow and mature to meet both our internal and external desires and dreams. By persevering and fulfilling our desires and dreams, we are truly etching our own individual trademarks of life in the sands of time on this earth.

Greg's Thoughts for Future Reflecting

1. *This would have been a good time for me to just give up, to throw in the towel.*

2. *A very strong and determined voice inside of me, sometimes whispering and sometimes very effectively shouting, caused me to listen.*

3. *Each of us possesses the inner power to slow down and listen to ourselves.*

Chapter Four

Listening
with a Limp

Desire alone is not enough.
But to lack desire means to lack a key
ingredient to success. Many a talented
individual failed because he lacked desire.
Many victories have been snatched by the
underdog because the underdog wanted it more.
So if you desire intensely and you act upon it,
then everything stands within your reach.
— ANONYMOUS

■ 27

The driving energy on my path of life was ever moving forward. I was now all of five years old, moving with the determination and fervor of a playful puppy. After three years of constant therapy, both in and out of the hospital, my growing legs were permanently freed from the leg braces that had become so much a part of my very being. For the first time since the crash, I was able to walk on my own and play without restraint.

This isn't to say that I was developing normally. My left leg showed visible signs of being more developed than my right leg, which was permanently affected by the crushing paralysis caused by the crash. The left side of my body had in fact become more dominant. Thanks to the crash, between the ages of two and five I switched from being right-handed in everything I did to becoming a proficient left-hander. I threw a baseball with my left hand, ate meals with my left hand, and worked with tools using my left hand. In short, I began to predominantly use my left hand, while my right hand became the helping hand in supporting the efforts of my left-handed activities.

Since my right leg was also shorter than my left, I walked with a slight limp, at times more pronounced than at others. My life seemed to be evolving around doing a number of things while walking with a limp, including now the ability to "listen with a limp."

This began to be a very interesting characteristic of my overall makeup. I not only carried with me an inner desire to want to learn, I moreover learned best by witnessing and listening to the living examples I encountered day by day. I spent my youthful days limping and hobbling around as I walked from place to place, constantly listening and learning from my own life experiences and also from those I came into contact with. Thus, the phrase "Listen with a limp" became a predominant characteristic and trademark of my life.

My physical abilities met the parameters of what was necessary to attend elementary school in a normal kindergarten setting. So, after taking a series of mental tests to determine whether a child is ready to enter school which I passed with flying colors, I prepared to begin school.

This readiness was accompanied by my family's move to a new house, a new neighborhood, a new elementary school (only some two blocks away from home), and a fresh new start for all of us, including my now two-year-old baby brother, Ken. Ken was a definite important addition to all our lives. He was another positive sign for my parents on their journey to success and life's fulfillment. And for me, Ken played an integral part in my life by being a support mechanism and companion. I now had a brother I could share my life with, including playing with toys and games, competitively fighting, romping around as brothers do, and sharing in family activities.

This new neighborhood also brought with it all types of opportunities for me to meet an abundant number of kids. In my kindergarten and first grade years, I became good friends with nine or ten of the kids who all lived within a two-block radius of my home. Some of these friendships lasted until I graduated from high school and a few remained until after I completed college.

It was a good feeling. I was full of anticipation and joy, and my parents were understandably anxious for me to do well in kindergarten and in many grade levels ahead.

While the strenuous events from years two to five left permanent marks on my life, both physically and emotionally, I enjoyed not only kindergarten but all the grade levels. Year by year, the experiences of the period before entering school in my life slowly faded away, becoming buried tragic memories of the past.

What helped to bury these memories was that at age five my parents began telling me that I was never to mention my past to anyone. I wasn't to share any recollections concerning the crash, my physical behaviors, or the leg braces I had worn for years.

Why? These were the 1950s and America was blossoming in the aftermath of World War II. Hitler and the Nazis had been crushed and the detention centers in the U.S. had been dismantled and dissolved. However, a certain attitude about physically and mentally handicapped children prevailed throughout our country. The government mandated that these types of children be sent to special schools for the abnormal and become institutionalized wards of the state.

For my parents, the very thought of me taking any other course in life than being brought up in a normal educational setting was out of the question. However, since we feared what might happen should my story ever be exposed, our silence was what you might call a joint family decision to ensure my successful future. This silence was added to my parents' already long list of obstacles and roadblocks to overcome.

Thus, this chapter of my life came to a close. The events and circumstances of the tragic car crash and its aftermath became deeply sealed away in the minds of those individuals most intimately involved. Those years were tucked away and were never brought up in any kind of conversation with friends or acquaintances.

However, the following five lessons I learned from this tragic event would never be forgotten and would remain part of the structure of my own personal trademark of life.

FIVE LESSONS EVOLVING FROM THE CRASH

1. Life is very fragile and can be swept away in an instant without even a moment's notice.
2. Live life to its fullest each day. Make the hours in each day important and meaningful to you.
3. Live life to its fullest each day with others. Make the hours you spend with others take on meaningful and relationship-building dimensions.
4. Never give up on being the best you desire to be in life through focusing on persevering, being determined, and following through despite the odds and roadblocks that are laid down before you on your path of life.
5. Be thankful, on a daily basis, for the many good people on this earth who touch and help to reinforce your life.

At the time, burying the past was good for me. Possessing the freedom to move about freely, experience life's many growth opportunities, and being allowed to create and explore were wonderful. All of these liberties became significant dimensions of my growth and being able to think for myself.

However, later on in my life, at about age thirty-five, it became quite apparent that I had a message to share with others. As a professional speaker, consultant, and writer who focuses on effective listening, my story has helped to encourage individuals in audiences from coast to coast and even around the world to accept how very important their attitude is so crucial in accomplishing anything worth pursuing in life. It's also a crucial component in the development of perfecting the art of effective listening. As I continue to speak to audiences, always walking to the platform with a limp, I constantly encourage a strong and determined attitude and I also reflect on how this ties into how to utilize the power of effective listening.

The limp and listening have become one, an integral part of my very being and existence upon this earth today. I'll forever be delivering the critical message of effective listening while limping from platform to platform and presenting the same message on each platform to audiences ranging from five people to ten thousand-plus individuals. In some of these audiences certain participants will even exclaim that I am teaching *them* how to listen with a limp. I don't mind, because I know that my message is starting to stick.

When confronted as a youth and teenager as to why I was walking with a limp, I merely explained that either I had a sprained ankle, a stiff leg from playing or exercising, or an injured knee. That explanation would usually end the discussion and it wasn't brought up again. For, you see, I was not about to become a victim or captive of my past. I wasn't about to continue to wear braces on my leg—literally *or* figuratively.

Where are you in your life today? When was the last time you slowed down long enough to take a personal inventory of where you are on your path of life? When was the last time you listened to what your inner self was really trying to express? What actions have you taken in response to these inner messages you received?

Free yourself from the braces in your life. Eliminate those barriers that are prohibiting you from achieving your personal success. Begin to listen to yourself in identifying the braces—the barriers—that are holding you back.

Enjoying the freedom to grow is a magnificent gift.

Greg's Thoughts for Future Reflecting

1. *Where are you in your life today?*
2. *When was the last time you slowed down long enough to take a personal inventory of where you are on your path of life?*
3. *Free yourself from the braces in your life.*

Chapter Five

Opportunities Become Accomplishments

*Accomplishments will prove
to be a journey, not a destination.*
– DWIGHT D. EISENHOWER

For every opportunity that arises in life, there also arise many options. I've had many choices to make and options to pursue in the fifty-plus years I've enjoyed since the crash. Looking back, I've identified some significant landmarks in my life where I've turned opportunities into accomplishments. These accomplishments not only benefited me, they also helped me to make a significant positive impact on others.

I've identified these significant points in my life to help me understand more clearly just how these accomplishments became landmarks, points of identification where I could show myself, not anyone else, that "I can do it." That driving internal listening mechanism was alive and well, forever helping me listen to myself. Since the crash, the ongoing need to show myself that I could accomplish tasks had become part of my inner character. One other significant matter that inspired me to accomplish various tasks was that these accomplishments would, in the long run, benefit others.

One of these significant landmarks began to take on its own identity when I joined the Cub Scouts in elementary school. This was a thoroughly enjoyable challenge, and the next logical step in this experience was to explore the challenges of the Webelos Scout. This began for me a strong disciplined program of accepting responsibility for any actions I took. These positive experiences solidified for me that I was going to continue my Scouting adventure, and in the sixth grade I became a Boy Scout, progressively working my way up and through the ranks.

Despite whatever physical challenges confronted me in accomplishing one task after another, I never looked at them as barriers or roadblocks. Some of these challenges included my actively doing push-ups, sit-ups, hiking, canoeing, knot tying, and walking through forests with thick underbrush. The challenge was that my right hand was not coordinated enough to instantly handle some situations, while my right leg and foot were weaker at times than my left leg and foot, and that slowed me down. Also, my limping became more pronounced at times. I always considered these challenges as steppingstones by taking one step at a time.

Then came the day when I achieved the ranking of Life Scout. To reach this rank is a great accomplishment in itself. The ranking of Life Scout is a steppingstone to the next ranking of Eagle Scout, the highest designation to be achieved in Boy Scouts. Friends who had shared in my Scouting enthusiasm up until this point seemed to be easing back, but I was more driven than ever to proceed and overcome the challenges that future merit badges and related activities had to offer.

When I was thirteen, I achieved the highest ranking in the Boy Scouts of America, the ranking of Eagle Scout. Only a very small percentage of all the Boy Scouts in the country ever obtain this rank. While achieving this honor at such a young age, I also completed the swimming and life-saving merit badge requirements. I continued on and received a palm for additional merit badges received. Additionally, I had the brief experience of serving as an assistant troop leader and continued my Scouting experience in a successful Explorer unit until I went off to college.

My Scouting experience made a dramatic impact on me, serving as a landmark that not only showed I was still very much alive, it also glowed as the symbol showing my inner need to persevere and accomplish a life's pursuit.

Being an Eagle Scout has made a big difference in how I carry myself as an adult. My guidelines for living follow the principles of the Scout Oath and the Scout Laws. These are not just a number of great words, they have become for me the very foundation to live by. Though the life of an Eagle Scout is not always an easy one, the Eagle pursues efforts in life with a commitment to responsibility and strong moral values. Character, honor, and values are the fiber that Eagle Scouts and those who pursue the Boy Scout adventure are molded from to meet life's many and varied challenges.

During these years when I was involved in Scouting, from age eleven to eighteen, my dad's daily efforts were primarily entrenched in supporting his family, first by working as a full-time firefighter. This involved being at work for one twenty-four-hour period, off for one twenty-four-hour period, on again for another twenty-four-hour period, and then off for a three-day period. Our family's lifestyle often revolved around my dad's firefighter's work schedule. Some mornings the family conversation over breakfast, upon my dad's return home from a twenty-four-hour tour of duty, would involve such subjects as how my dad went into a burning house, down the basement stairs into a smoke-filled basement, and successfully shut off the exposed gas meter to a leaking line. Other episodes included how he and his team of firefighters had manned and fought an industrial fire for the past twelve to eighteen hours. Yet other episodes included how his team had entered a burning house or industrial building and had avoided becoming victims to the caving-in floors around them. Oftentimes, over breakfast, we'd find my dad sitting at the kitchen table with dirty, smoke-ridden work clothes after just getting off a twenty-four-hour tour, and a lot of times getting little sleep. On my dad's off hours he would take care of chores around the house, spend time with my mom and us boys, and work a few hours a week at his investment advisory business.

During this time, my mom would continue to take care of the daily household tasks, look after the upbringing of my brother, Ken, and myself, and manage the family budget and its operations.

My brother, Ken, led a normal and fulfilling life as a youth. He played and socialized with other kids at school and in the neighborhood. He enjoyed a life barrier free from any major physical or mental interventions. I was happy for his everyday achievements and participation in life.

Though our parents made sure that both my brother and I were baptized, our religious upbringing was that of a freedom to practice and believe but with no commitment to any particular church or religion. To the best of my recollections, my parents never practiced any particular religion or attended church, except at weddings and funerals. The only discussion I ever heard about this matter was that the trauma of the war, its aftermath, and the car crash had a definite impact upon the religious part of my parents' lives.

Even so, we had a wooden crucifix that hung in a prominent place in our living room during the years of our growing up. My parents called themselves non-practicing Christians—ones who believed, but didn't attend any church.

On our own, my brother, Ken, and I infrequently attended a non-denominational Christian church about three blocks away from our home. Our parents never prompted or encouraged us to attend services, but as I became more committed to the character-building attributes of the Boy Scout program, I became more committed to this non-denominational church's religious education programs and to attending services. Later in my teen years, this same and even stronger commitment transferred to the Lutheran church where a number of my friends worshiped. Throughout my later high school days and when I came back home from college, I attended and practiced the beliefs of the Lutheran church.

At age eighteen, with my feet firmly planted in this foundation, I moved away from my parents to Western Michigan University. My transition to college life in the first two months caused me to have mixed feelings. On the one hand there existed some apprehensiveness over meeting new friends in the dorm and in classes, along with getting acquainted with the professors and adjusting to the independent class structure. Also, the amount of studying that was demanded of me increased tenfold over that expected in high school.

On the other hand, I began to enjoy socializing with a number of male and female students in classes, in the student union facility, in the dorm, and at various campus functions. I made several close and lasting friendships with these students, and I began to sprout my own wings and to form my own individual identity. This was exciting. However, I never confided in anyone about the crash until I met the woman who later became my wife. And other than her, I never confided in anyone else for years.

I found myself walking for miles at a time across campus. Sometimes I was limping more profoundly than others, but somehow I always kept walking. At times, I would actually be hobbling. After all this walking, I would be more tired than my friends, but I hardly ever commented on my condition. As usual, if one of my friends asked about my condition, I wrote it off as either a sprained ankle or an injured knee from sports involvement.

I attended classes regularly and became a communications major with an emphasis on teaching. Once again my inner drive took over and I attended classes almost year around in order to acquire a degree. Traditionally, students took fall and winter courses, left campus in April, and returned in late August. Again, that internal listening mechanism was receiving loud messages from my inner driving force that said these extra spring and sometimes summer efforts were absolutely necessary initiatives I desired to pursue.

While I was pursuing my educational goals, I became a member of the Beta Sigma Psi fraternity, worked in several capacities at the campus radio station, assisted in putting on performances at Western's newly-built Shaw Theater, and was a part of the Campus Disciplinary Board.

I also had the opportunity to assist in the campus Lutheran Church, first as an usher, then in helping to prepare the church and altar, and eventually as an assistant to the minister at the services. During my years on this college campus, my relationship grew with the Lutheran pastor, Dr./Reverend Paul Maier. Reverend Maier was a dedicated Lutheran minister and also a history professor on Western's campus and became my spiritual leader and mentor. He wrote *First Christmas, Pontius Pilate,* and many other books and inspirational writings. The knowledge and wisdom I drew from my experiences with Reverend Maier have become a landmark within a landmark on my path of life.

Again, reminders of the breathing blanket appeared in this landmark within a landmark. These reminders once again reflected off the very much alive breathing blanket and my very existence on this earth in the following ways:

■ You and I have the power to design, shape, and live our lives by pursuing the many magnificent opportunities that God provides us daily–despite the odds.

- You and I have the ability to utilize the power of effective listening so that we can recognize these magnificent opportunities.

- You and I also possess the inner ability to act upon these opportunities by utilizing the energies captured in our hearts, minds, and souls.

- Most importantly, you and I have the ability to live rich and rewarding lives where "opportunities become accomplishments."

As my college days came to a close, graduation was about to become another significant landmark, for I graduated in just three years with certified teaching credentials. I was continuing to show myself that I could do it, that I could accomplish anything I set out to despite the odds of the crash that affected me physically and mentally.

Shortly after my graduation from college, I accepted a teaching position as a Communications Instructor in a high school in the West Michigan area, yet another landmark in my life.

All told, these landmarks were significant measures of my very existence and well-being here on this earth, for throughout my growing-up years, renowned doctors and specialists had continued to warn my parents and me that lingering effects of the crash were still present in the mobility, coordination, and usage of my right hand, leg, and foot. As mentioned before, I was told in my late teens to make the most of life in the next twenty years because at that point my body and mind would begin to deteriorate and I would eventually become an invalid and die in a wheelchair.

Each time, after hearing the thoughts and long-range prognosis of these specialists, my first inclination was to despair. The explanations sounded so convincing that the projections of my future were difficult to refute. During these encounters and their immediate aftermaths, I became blinded and disoriented. Momentarily, the wind would be sucked out of my sails. I remember moments of internally screaming out in pain and denial, "This is not the way. Find me. Help me, Guiding Light." The physical and emotional pain endured during these moments desecrated my inner strength and abilities

However, in the days and weeks to follow each of these death-defying encounters of a different kind, my inner being adjusted and disciplined patterns took hold. Once again, my innermost being would become my guiding light that reflected so beautifully off the "breathing blanket."

This guiding light of imagination and wonder would recapture my attention and once again I would find myself journeying, living, and enjoying the miracles that were offered. Once again, I would tell myself that I was not going to allow medical specialists to determine my destiny. My life's plans, triumphs, and accomplishments were going to be determined by me. *I* would be free to breathe the freshness that life had to offer. *I* possessed the freedom to pursue the challenges of my own life, and opportunities continued to be accomplished.

Greg's Thoughts for Future Reflecting

1. *These transitions not only benefited me, they also helped me to make a significant positive impact on others.*

2. *Being an Eagle Scout has made a big difference in how I carry myself as an adult.*

3. *You and I have the ability to utilize the power of effective listening so that we can recognize these magnificent opportunities.*

Chapter Six

An "I Can Do It" Attitude

*Creativity has been built into every one of us;
it's part of our design. Each of us lives less of
the life God intended for us when we choose
not to live out the creative powers we possess.*
— TED ENGSTROM

*A*t the young age of twenty-one, I was beginning to discover the meaning of living in the real adult world. I was ready to embrace and encounter the challenges of the working world after doing my student teaching and graduating from college. I felt that I was now prepared to either become a communications teacher or to work in the corporate world.

An overwhelming "I can do it" attitude sprang up daily as a true motivating factor, bringing excitement and encouragement into my path of life. As I have thought about the common denominator that helped me to establish each of my landmarks, it's this "I can do it" attitude. Not only did it become part of my everyday method of operation, it was especially helpful when overcoming some real roadblocks to reaching my final goals.

I became so determined to reach each of these goals that I refused to accept "No." Even when some of my best friends, relatives, and medical specialists were trying to convince me that I should give up or quit trying to succeed or get ahead, this "I can do it" attitude took hold. I was in high gear with this powerful momentum carrying me forward to complete each task at hand, though sometimes internal struggles required an extra measure of physical and/or mental exertion and endurance.

The doors to the world were wide open, and the foundation to pursue my path of life was intact and ready for growth and experimentation. This foundation consisted of several important components, the first and most important being meeting, courting, and marrying my beautiful wife, Anna, who had become a significant partner in the rest of my life by the time I graduated from college.

My foundation or launching pad to my continuing path of life also included the significant factor that I actually graduated from college. I received a Bachelor of Arts degree and diploma from Western Michigan University in communications and education. I also, amazingly, completed this accomplishment in three years, including my student teaching, compared to most college students with whom I graduated who more traditionally completed their degrees in four to five years.

With this new foundation, the ties became severed between my tentative, devastating, and non-reassuring past on the east side of the state and my newly emerging, positive, assertive, and meaningful future on the west side of the state.

This "I can do it" attitude was now more alive than ever and was even more pronounced than during my teen years, as my actions and goals were now being perceived from an adult perspective and direction. Without exception, I found that if a goal was worth accomplishing I invested 100 to 120 percent of the time, energy, and effort needed to complete the task and do it well.

Some of the significant goals that emerged on this launching pad included:

- keeping and maintaining an open mind to allow creativity to keep entering my life,
- keeping and maintaining an open mind to allow new ideas to evolve and mature,
- building a future on a day-by-day basis where opportunities could develop into real-life accomplishments.

On the other hand, some of the significant roadblocks that emerged on this launching pad included:

- wondering how far I could go before my physical limitations actually brought my progress to a definite stop,
- wondering how my moments of complacency would affect my overall attitude of being creative and forever developing,

▪ wondering how I would handle and treat my failures and shortcomings while encountering the opportunities on my path of life.

My final resolve to these many questions was and remains that I would pursue each challenge and opportunity I was confronted with by taking them one at a time with intense passion and focus. Along with this effort, and drawing on the partnering power of God in my heart and soul, I forged forward with my pursuits and commitments. I also held myself accountable for my own actions. This began the very moment I entered the adult world of working at age twenty-one.

In today's working world, twenty and even thirty-year-olds are taught that their world is evolving around them and that they'll probably have ten to twelve different jobs in their lifetimes, and actively participate in as many as five to seven career changes. They are also being told that this is healthy and will be the accepted norm of the future.

Well, my past thirty-plus years in the working world have reflected these trends. I have found myself being twenty years ahead of my time, and I don't regret one moment of experiencing these many real-life opportunities.

My first real-world career/job/endeavor was as a communications teacher and coach at a West Michigan high school. By sharing in this opportunity, my students became better communicators of the spoken and listened-to word.

During my days as a high school communications instructor, I kept and maintained a creative open mind in my pursuit to help these students master the art of being able to express their thoughts and emotions in a constructive and understandable way. I also built a separate Communications Department, directed two to three play productions per year, pursued a Masters Degree in Communications and Education, and developed and taught an advanced communications curriculum at this high school.

When my ideals and those of the high school principal began to clash, my life was faced with pursuing another career. I thus ventured out to become successful in the business world. I was looking forward to the many challenges and opportunities that I was about to encounter and pursue.

I first accepted becoming a multi-department store manager with one of the large national chain department stores. I enjoyed the experience of dealing with an abundant number of challenges and overcoming limitations in working with people and merchandise handling. This was not going to become my life's pursuit, but it definitely proved to be a growth experience on my path of life.

I then ventured out to pursue further life experiences and landed in the insurance sales industry, becoming involved in property-casualty insurance and life insurance efforts. I enjoyed helping other people with their insurance needs for several years, but became dismayed with the sales tactics that were promoted by the management and that ran against my moral and ethical values. So, another growth opportunity in the business world came and went and the educational process continued. Toward the end of my insurance career a new manager came aboard, and I actually enjoyed my last few months in insurance. My sales figures actually increased as I was on my way out. Whatever the case may have been, the driving and creative force reflecting off the breathing blanket was telling me to move on in life, to meet other challenges and opportunities. So, I listened to the message and allowed myself to encounter yet another life experience.

After a little soul searching and reevaluation of my future pursuits, an opportunity appeared in our local school system. This was a one-year position subsidized by the Federal Government acting as a Career Education Facilitator. My responsibilities involved informing and implementing a culture of total career awareness in the everyday curriculum structure from kindergarten through the twelfth grade. This effort included helping students determine where their major interests existed, what type of working environments they would succeed best in, and what types of educational commitments it would take to meet their future expectations. I felt somewhat prepared to pursue this effort, especially after completing two or three courses in career education in my masters program.

As with any challenge in life for me, I pursued this as another life opportunity and with total commitment in my daily communications with the superintendent, the school principals, and the teachers throughout the elementary schools, junior high, and high school. Once again I found myself in a position where I was assisting others to improve their way of life. I also found this position to be a pleasant sabbatical between being involved in the insurance industry and continuing with the adventures on the remainder of my path of life. I also had the opportunity to resolve these real-life adventures with my wife, Anna, who shared in my everyday ups and downs, frustrations, and celebrations.

As the years progressed, I continued to enjoy being involved in the areas of sales and relationship building, and also in management. I also became acquainted with the different business principles, disciplines, and practices of many businesses and organizations first by working in the office automation industry.

Ultimately, I became a territory manager with a large Fortune 500 pharmaceutical research company. Throughout the next decade I utilized my inner talent to work effectively in sales, sales training, marketing projects, research and development, management, and international sales consulting. My goals and efforts were, as always, set at the 120 percent level. For the majority of these years, my efforts received Sales Elite national recognition as one of the nation's top ten producers in the country. This national recognition served as a sign of my success in the business world as well as an internal measure of satisfaction that I was alive and making a difference in helping others succeed.

The glimmering ray of light was once again reflecting off the breathing blanket and guiding me to help others succeed, and I continued to follow the moral values and sound character-building attributes that I had learned in my days of Scouting and from the Holy Bible.

My experiences in Toastmasters International bear this out. I'll always be proud of my relationship with this non-profit, voluntary international organization that is dedicated to helping people from all walks of life all over the world improve their leadership and communications skills. As I strived to help others become leaders, the breathing blanket was not only telling me "I can do it," it was directing me to use my morals, values, and character-building attributes as I communicated with others and made decisions. This meant working through many thoughts and ideas in the preparation and delivery of presentations, both at the club and district levels, to many different audiences, always with a message to help others succeed.

This also meant a commitment of time in helping others create and establish new clubs where individuals could receive the same gift that I received in improving their communications and leadership skills.

Ultimately, I attained the highest international achievement in Toastmasters International, that of Distinguished Toastmaster (DTM). Acquiring my DTM became another significant landmark, serving as another dynamic "I can do it."

A key factor that made this landmark even more significant was that all the tasks I had to accomplish to acquire my DTM were pursued in the years after my fortieth birthday. By this time, by all medical calculations, I was supposed to be in a wheelchair awaiting my demise.

I also helped out the leadership efforts of this organization in several capacities on the district level as well as a District Governor. It's been a heart-warming and enriching experience to see many a Toastmaster start out by presenting their icebreaker presentation, actively participate in the program over the next six months to a year, and become a more confident and helpful individual in just a brief period of time.

How are you utilizing the motivating catalysts in your everyday activities? My key motivating catalyst is the ever-constant reminder of the breathing blanket. Think about it, if the blanket had never started breathing, we wouldn't be having this very exchange of ideas today. Another significant factor that reminds me of the breathing blanket is that every time I get up and start walking I can physically, and always with a mental awareness, feel that I am limping. Sometimes my foot and leg are more painful than at other moments. There are also moments when my right foot will turn inward and I'll be walking on the side of my foot. This painful and challenging method of walking sometimes lasts for a couple of days, and many times throughout the past fifty-plus years this condition has lasted for weeks at a time. For, you see, this whole idea of walking serves as way more than just a simple pinch or nudge; it serves as a wake-up call and a reminder of the breathing blanket. This constant alarm is a reminder to pursue life "in the spirit of sharing with others daily." This ever-enduring power is derived from an inner practiced strength of an inner ability to utilize the power of effective listening.

Have you slowed down enough so that you can start to identify your motivating catalysts? What are your symbols of hope? Take a moment to listen to yourself. If you do this, you will find yourself conferring with your own morals, values, and character-building attributes. Routinely listen to yourself so that you can begin to identify the landmarks on your own path of life. These will add moments of strength and enrichment to your everyday activities and you, too, will find that you can exceed life's expectations by listening to the teachings revealed by your own landmarks.

Greg's Thoughts for Future Reflecting

1. *An overwhelming "I can do it" attitude sprang up daily as a true motivating factor, bringing excitement and encouragement into my path of life.*

2. *Without exception, I found that if a goal was worth accomplishing, I invested 100 to 120 percent of the time, energy, and effort needed to complete the task and do it well.*

3. *How are you utilizing the motivating catalysts in your everyday activities?*

Chapter Seven

The Perpetually Evolving Landmark

*People today hunger to be listened to,
and they reward those who give them the
respect of effective listening with loyalty,
cooperation, and the willingness
to see others' points of view.*
– GREG BAUER, "GURU OF LISTENING"

*L*andmarks are not brief moments in time. They are not established overnight. They do not provide mere instant gratification. The landmarks I am describing involve a number of events that have been successfully accomplished. They involve an investment of energy over a long period of time, not only years but in some cases even decades of focus, commitment, and dedication.

Furthermore, over time, these landmarks have helped me define my inner belief in myself and also my belief in others, which in turn has led me to ask myself if I've been making a positive difference in others' lives. This key component of possessing an internal desire to serve others becomes very significant in establishing and maintaining an innovative and life-building attitude at work, at home, in community activities and volunteerism, and at play. Both mentally and intellectually, I find myself the happiest and most fulfilled when I'm helping others to succeed on their path of life.

This feeling and understanding brings about a sense of purpose and meaning as to my very existence on this earth since the crash at age two. Each time I help another individual or actively listen to another's joy or plight in life, I do not question the moment but celebrate the many opportunities that God has handed me in his own special way. Ultimately, these opportunities are gifts of life from above that I have, over the years, learned to accept and act upon in God's name.

The next and final landmark in my life is the most significant and the most cherished landmark of all the landmarks put together. It is a perpetually evolving landmark that keeps nourishing and strengthening my inner soul and well being. I'm very excited about sharing with you this very special aspect of my path of life. Where should I begin?

Well, during my college years, I dated several different young ladies, but these all ended up being brief superficial encounters. Other relationships with college-aged females were purely supportive friendships.

Then, in my later years of college, I became involved in a special relationship with an extraordinary young and beautiful college-aged lady, Anna. We met over breakfast one early Sunday morning before church in a dining room that was between the two dormitories we resided in on campus. We began to see each other daily and dated exclusively for the next eleven months. During this period of our getting to know each other and of our engagement, another significant transition was taking place that affected our lives. We both shared a strong and deep belief in God, and that God would play a significant role in our lives now and in the future. Allow me to explain the spiritual opportunity that unfolded.

As I became better acquainted with Anna's upbringing in Battle Creek, Michigan, I realized that her entire religious background was Catholic. I had no positive or negative impressions or education concerning Catholicism. Anna had attended Catholic schools from the first grade on into high school and had even attended her first year of college at an all-girls Catholic college. Also, I discovered that her entire extended family, on both sides, followed and actively practiced Catholicism.

For a six-month period we attended church two times every Sunday: one Lutheran service and one Catholic Mass. We were attempting to come to a mutual decision as to which religious beliefs we were going to follow and utilize in our marriage.

Also, during this six-month period, I began to take religious information classes at the campus Catholic Church that we attended in order to acquire a clearer understanding of the Catholic Church's principles and services. For you see, the couple of times that I had visited a Catholic Mass in my earlier college days, I hadn't been sure what I was really seeing or experiencing. These classes helped me develop a much clearer view of the Mass and of Catholic beliefs. Surprisingly, I found many similarities with Lutheran practices.

While I was becoming educated and informed about Catholicism, Anna was likewise becoming enlightened as to Lutheran principles.

When the time came to make the decision as to which religious practices we were going to share as a married couple, we both compromised and acquiesced to each other's desires. We also conferred with the Lutheran Minister Reverend Paul Maier, who advised us to follow the direction of our hearts and minds. However, he also conveyed that my converting to Catholicism would mean his giving up any future aspirations he held for me in becoming a Lutheran minister.

After more consideration and reflection, I came to the ultimate decision to make the conversion to Catholicism and that we would consummate our vows of marriage in the Catholic Church. This we did, in the universal eyes of God. This one special moment in our lives was a true celebration of our perpetually evolving landmark. This very special day became the launching point of our journey in life together in God's eyes and also in the eyes of all the hundreds of individuals we would encounter in our lifetimes. We've been very pleased with our decision for many years. In the spirit of my need to serve others, which had been a take-off of Reverend Maier's teachings, I continued serving, only now in a different church, the Catholic Church, all in God's name. Throughout the past thirty-plus years, I've served as a member of the Parish Board, chaired the Parish Board, served on the Liturgy Commission, chaired the Liturgy Commission, headed up the facilitators of the Masses who assist the priests in preparing for the Masses, and still continue to serve as a Eucharistic Minister. So, I have continued to serve the people of the church of God, perhaps just not as I had originally thought I would.

I had become attracted and attached to Anna's moral and spiritual values, to her genuine interest in our mutual activities and love for each other, and to our commitment to sharing a lifetime together. This beautiful young lady, in all of life's gifted dimensions, accepted me with all her heart and soul. Anna took my background as a part of her own and made the commitment to join me in facing life's choices, challenges, roadblocks, opportunities, and accomplishments. I also accepted the commitment of life together as one with my own heart and soul.

Over the months before our marriage, I described in full detail to Anna the night of the crash, my emotional and physical past, and the medical specialists' prognosis for my future and the challenges we'd have to face together in marriage. Bless her, she loved me for who I was and for whatever life we would create together in God's eyes.

We gave birth to three wonderful children–Matthew, Jennifer, and Angela. We've lovingly invested thousands of hours into their well being and their life's aspirations, always fully realizing that they are establishing their own life's opportunities, pursuits, and accomplishments. Anna and I also have our own separate job aspirations and we share a strong belief in supporting each other's career choices. Our ever-constant belief in ourselves and each other's ability to succeed remains a powerful driving force. This holds true in establishing and maintaining any relationship, whether it involves marriage, business, or social conditions.

Throughout our three-plus decades of marriage, we've encountered many challenges and roadblocks. Our life together has not been exclusively joyous, but we've experienced countless truly beautiful moments together. We try to meet our daily activities and challenges head on with a positive attitude and outlook.

Also, throughout these years, we've learned to adjust, compensate, and compromise with my physical challenges and limitations. Anna has always been very supportive of the things I can do and does not focus on the things I can't do. I've consistently tried to realize the world from the same perspective, though it goes without saying that I've experienced many a moment of absolute mental and/or physical frustration and Anna has served as my rock and foundation, urging me to always move forward.

Some of these frustrations and limitations have occurred over the past twenty years, when my right leg, being significantly shorter and thinner than my left, throbs with pain. Sometimes this pain occurs in my right foot, at other times in my upper right leg or hip, or sometimes in my lower right leg. This stunning pain can also occur in more than one place at a time. It can strike from just sitting or standing for a period of ten minutes or more at one given time, to walking (with a limp) for too long.

By walking with this limp, my entire body's alignment is constantly being shifted, causing my entire spine to become misaligned. This way of walking also brings about tensed lower back, shoulder, and neck muscles. It also limits the amount of physical activity that I can perform on any given day. I continue to walk on the right side of my right foot with my ankle internally tying itself up into a knotted-up ball of screaming fire. When sitting in my leisure chair, trying to relax, my tense right foot, ankle, and entire right leg begin to twitch, flutter, and vibrate uncontrollably. This condition continues for as long as fifteen to thirty minutes or until I physically get up, walk around a bit, and return to trying to relax again by returning to my chair and possibly doing some deep-breathing exercises. Lately I've had Anna massage my tense, twitching legs. Believe me, it helps to momentarily relieve some of the tension and pain.

The only other relief I obtain from this total state of tension and pain is from my regular visits to see a chiropractor. Since age forty, Dr. Paul Sarver and, more recently, Dr. Eric Lambert have helped my body mend and heal itself through the use of the activator method of chiropractic medicine. Chiropractic medicine has proven to be a lifesaver of an alternative form of medicine that consistently helps my body readjust after I misalign it through my daily activities and from constantly walking with a limp.

You see, my strong will to succeed, pursue, and persevere lies deep inside and is expressed daily. The need to move, breathe, and be alive are all internal and external messages sent by the breathing blanket that I continue to receive. A strong will, focus, and energy to perform are very much alive. These far outweigh the physical pain and mental anguish I've experienced. My ever-loving Anna, my perpetually evolving landmark, is there every day to remind me that the blanket is very much alive.

She's also there to remind me of my ongoing mission in life to help others to utilize the power of effective listening in their daily activities to help them live, grow, and prosper by actively using their ears. My purpose and catalyst for staying alive is derived from the internal spirit to serve others, and to do this *without* painkilling drugs or liquor.

Each day provides another opportunity for me to reach down deep inside and share in the possibilities that life has to offer with my beautiful loving wife. She is truly my closest partner and companion on life's journey.

Each day also provides another opportunity for me to stretch my physical horizons, so I take walks and/or ride a bike, or walk behind a self-propelled walking lawn mower. Some days I can walk one or two miles, and some days I can only walk a city block at the most before I have to sit down and rest. Other days I can ride a bike only about a half-mile before my legs and tightened knees can go no further, whereas some days I've peddled for four or five miles and feel physically energized for a period of time. Some days I can only mow the front yard before my legs will go no further. Then, the backyard either waits to be mowed another day or Anna comes to complete the task.

As a professional speaker, I share the story of the breathing blanket to help my audiences identify with the importance of attitude in their own lives and of utilizing the power of effective listening. Moreover, I remind them that while I'm standing and moving around on the platform before them, this stunning pain inevitably will occur. I reinforce the fact that, when these moments occur, I focus all my energies on the message I'm attempting to convey and how I'm there to help them succeed and to celebrate their accomplishments, which helps greatly in diverting my attention from the pain.

As of the day of this writing, my wife and I are very much alive and enjoying the challenges and new frontiers that lie before us. We're also enjoying sharing with others in their everyday thoughts and challenges. Our own lives and indeed our marriage became so much more enriched by sharing in others' life experiences.

What of your marriage? Instead of investing a disproportionate amount of time focusing on the negative aspects of your marriage, invest more qualitative energies in discussing, dreaming, and focusing on the positives. For you see, the blanket may pay you a visit at the most inopportune time in your life. For most of us, this is also a time when its visit is least expected.

For this reason, it is important to invest in the five positive principles of living that I have developed:

FIVE POSITIVE PRINCIPLES OF LIVING

1. Believe–in yourself.
2. Believe–in your spouse.
3. Believe–in others.
4. Believe–in opportunities and emerging accomplishments.
5. Believe–in the spirit of the breathing blanket.

Allow your heart and soul to hold true to these beliefs. If you truly love and admire that special person in your life, begin to express your feelings, emotions, and purposes of intent today, and may the spirit of the breathing blanket prevail in the hearts and souls of each of you.

Your belief in yourself and your ability to succeed is vitally important if you are to achieve landmarks and celebrate accomplishments. Your belief in others and their abilities to succeed is even more important in helping them acquire their own life's aspirations.

Even today, despite those specialists' gloomy prognosis, I'm still eager to celebrate my ability to walk, always with a limp, each day. I'm also very eager to celebrate my ability and capacity to speak, listen to, and comprehend the many communications I encounter on a daily basis with individuals and audiences.

I thank God daily for providing me with the strength and inner ability to share with others my innermost dreams and life's mission in helping them understand how to utilize the power of effective listening in their everyday activities in their work, studying, socializing, and worshiping.

Throughout the past years, I have made my peace and amends with my maker, God the Almighty. I forgave the drunk driver years ago and made peace in my heart and soul with that issue. However, I will never be able to forget the crash and how it has affected my life and the lives of so many others. Yes, I have prepared my mind, heart, and soul for inevitable death here on this earth many times over. I'm very comfortable with my relationship with God. For you see, at age two when the blanket was placed over me, I had not received the opportunity to prepare myself for my final days. This time, I am prepared for God's final calling. Granted, there's no big hurry and I'm very much enjoying this precious time he's given me on this earth. I'm truly celebrating my abilities to help, serve, and share with others. However, my final calling will come and may occur in some other mysterious unexpected way. Who really knows?

Also, throughout the past many years, I've come to one particular realization in working with God and sharing with others here on earth. This discovery is so profound and yet so simple that I've recently shared it with my now grown children over some of our family meals together.

This simple realization revolves around how very important it is to keep in touch with our personal perspectives and balance of life. I discovered this by participating in church services on a weekly basis. My attendance helps me greatly in keeping a check on my own personal perspectives and life's balance in my pursuit of my aspirations. Sunday morning church services have become a special time for me to clear my mind of clutter and to acquire the ability to stimulate new creative and concrete thought patterns for the week ahead. You are encouraged to regularly attend your own place of worship

to obtain and maintain a more positive and broader outlook on life's many gifts and benefits.

You are a terrific and unique individual here on God's
earth with so many gifts and talents just waiting to be
shared with others. These gifts can best be visualized,
comprehended, and acted upon by increasing your ability
to utilize the power of effective listening, both internally
and externally. Constantly make sure that your listening
switch is in the "on" position when listening to your inner
thoughts and expressions, and also when working with
others in any life situations.

Also, find your positive attitude switch and constantly check it to be sure it too is in the "on" position. Yes,
it is that switch labeled "I can do it." You say it's in the
back room? Well, revive this switch and place it in the
forefront of every horizon in your mind.

The breathing blanket reminds us to take time each
day to celebrate life's many gifts and benefits.

You have the perseverance.

You have the determination.

You possess the ability to be that successful, creative,
and contributing individual that you desire to become
during your days here on this earth.

You can make the commitment to live life to its
fullest and start to lead an even more abundant lifestyle.

Welcome to my world: "In the spirit of sharing with
others, opportunities become accomplishments."

Greg's Thoughts for Future Reflecting

1. Over time, these landmarks have helped me define my inner belief in myself and also my belief in others, which in turn has led me to ask myself if I've been making a positive difference in others' lives.

2. This very special day became the launching point of our journey in life together in God's eyes and also in the eyes of all the hundreds of individuals we will encounter in our lifetime.

3. My ever-loving Anna, my perpetually evolving landmark, is there every day to remind me that the blanket is very much alive.

About the Author

Greg Bauer and his organization, Greg Bauer and Associates, Inc., are dedicated to helping others share in the life-long benefits received from enhancing their abilities to utilize the power of effective listening in their daily activities. Greg is very much committed to his vision of making active listening a worldwide reality.

As an international professional speaker, consultant, and author of proven communication and listening skills, ideas, and techniques, Greg Bauer helps others to discover the lost art of listening in their lives and provides them with the tools necessary to practice effective, active listening daily. His keynotes, workshops, and presentations have inspired thousands to make a difference in how they more effectively redefine their own personal measure in their communications with family members, and business and social acquaintances.

With vast experience in the educational and corporate arenas, Greg Bauer's leading edge mission in life is to enhance the communication behaviors in corporate sales, relationship building, customer service, and management with the methods of effective listening that he has developed over the past thirty years. He is resolute in his commitment to his mission that now also touches the lives of many in associations, churches, and universities.

In a very unique and compelling way Greg captures and inspires his audiences to maintain a positive mental attitude by sharing the emotions and life pursuits revealed in his signature story, *The Breathing Blanket*.

For a more in-depth look at Greg Bauer and the benefits you or your company can receive from his organization, you are encouraged to refer to his website: *www.listenone.com*.